Honiton

Past and Present

Chips Barber

Regards!
Chips Barber

Illustrations by
Jane Reynolds

GW00482902

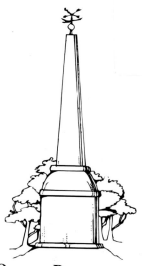

OBELISK PUBLICATIONS

Other Titles in This Series

Topsham Past and Present, *Chips Barber*
Sidmouth Past and Present, *Chips Barber*
Cullompton Past and Present, *Jane Leonard*
The Great Little Exeter Book, *Chips Barber*
The Great Little Dartmoor Book, *Chips Barber*
The Great Little Totnes Book, *Chips Barber*
The Great Little Plymouth Book, *Chips Barber*
The Great Little Chagford Book, *Chips Barber*

OTHER OBELISK PUBLICATIONS ABOUT THIS AREA

Ten Family Walks in East Devon, *Chips Barber*
Curiosities of East Devon, *Derrick Warren*
Around The Churches of East Devon, *Walter Jacobson*
Along The Otter, *Chips Barber*
Walks on and around Woodbury Common, *Chips Barber*
Exmouth in Colour, *Chips Barber*
Sidmouth in Colour, *Chips Barber*
Short Circular Walks in and around Sidmouth, *Chips Barber*

We have over 170 Devon-based titles, for a current list please send an s.a.e. to the address given below or telephone (01392) 468556.

ACKNOWLEDGEMENTS
Thanks to Mr A. Dimond, Mr D. Cooper and Mr Bill Crane for all their help.

First published in 2000 by
Obelisk Publications, 2 Church Hill, Pinhoe, Exeter, Devon
Designed by Chips and Sally Barber
Edited and Typeset by Sally Barber
Printed in Great Britain

Honiton

Past and Present

Although I'm not a native of the town, my memories and associations with Honiton are fond ones: I remember scoring my debut goal, as an eleven-year-old, in a 4-0 away win against Honiton Secondary Modern School and as an adult, or something approaching one, I recall my first teaching practice at the same school, then under the headship of Mr Badman, who wasn't too keen on 'long-haired students' like me! In the years since then my visits have been many and varied and I now feel I have learned enough about this industrious little town to want to share some of its fascinating history. Having tried photography on a number of occasions, I swiftly came to the conclusion that a book illustrated by drawings would be best. An artist has the licence to remove traffic (and traffic wardens, however pleasant and bilingual!), yellow lines, street 'furniture', market stalls, people, strong shadows and so on, all of which make the taking of good pictures difficult in Honiton. So, utilising the talents of local artist Jane Reynolds, I shall try to give a flavour of this ancient place which has, in recent years, become the 'antiques capital' of the region.

Black's Guide of 1891 had this as its entry for Honiton: *"We now cross the Chard and Exeter roads, and run to the market town of Honiton (population 3301). Inns; The Dolphin and Golden Lion – the latter traditionally reputed to have been the residence of the abbots of Dunkeswell … It occupies the slope of a pleasant valley, watered by the fish-abounding Otter, and is one of the prettiest, cleanest and most agreeable of Devonshire towns. Every lady in England is familiar with*

Honiton early in the 20th century

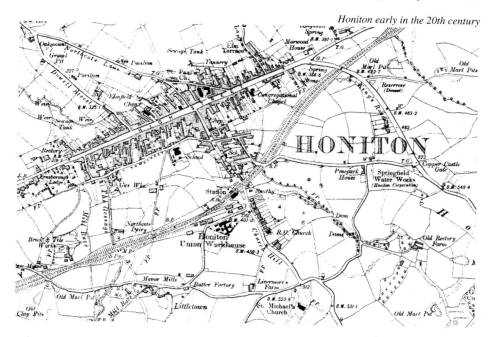

its rich and delicate handmade lace, of which the Queen's [Victoria] *bridal robe was fashioned; and the households of Dorset have long tasted the excellence of Honiton butter. The dairy produce of this fertile vale is also despatched to the London markets. The lace manufacture was introduced here by the Lollards in the reign of Elizabeth* [the First!].

Honiton has two 'parish' churches – St Paul's, built in 1837, containing a good copy of Raffaelle's "Transfiguration" for its altarpiece – and the old parish church of St Michael, occupying the high ground south of the town. The latter was a priory chapel, built by Bishop Courtenay in 1484, and contains a graceful oaken screen, which is unhappily disfigured with paint, and the black marble tomb of Thomas Marwood, physician to Queen Elizabeth, who practised physics for seventy-five years, and died at the age of 105. A successful cure for an ailing Earl of Essex raised him into eminence, and his sovereign rewarded him with a gift of land at Widworthy. His son (also "a leech") built a house in Honiton, which is still standing, and which sheltered Charles I on the night of the 25th of July 1644.

The view from the churchyard is extensive, and embraces the meanderings of the crystal Otter; the long straggling street of Honiton, watered by a pleasant brook ..."

This is how the somewhat gushing *The Book of Fair Devon*, published in 1899–1900, saw some of Honiton's other attractions. *"Amongst the many places of interest in the beautiful county of Devon, Honiton may fairly claim to be remembered. Those who have never visited Honiton have at least heard of Honiton lace and the lace trade is in a vigorous and improving state at the present time. Visitors who approach Devonshire by the London and South Western Railway cannot fail to notice the pleasant situation of the town in the valley of the Otter. The wooded hill of St Cyres is a notable feature of the landscape. Honiton is one of the many charming little spots in England which have never been much advertised, in spite of their attractions. The town is really little more than one broad street. The country is very near at hand on either side. Here, if anywhere, is* rus in urbe *– town and country – side by side. It is said that Honiton is in the valley of the Otter, but, to speak more accurately, it lies on the slope of one of the hills which form the valley, a hundred feet above the Otter and from three hundred to five hundred feet above the sea.*

To visitors who are satisfied with the pursuits of country life, the town and neighbourhood have many attractions. The walks in the vicinity are almost inexhaustible, and it would be difficult to hit upon a walk or drive that would be dull or monotonous. The heights of Dumdonn [sic] *and Hembury Fort, with their old Roman and other camps, the Axminster road, Marl Pits Hill, the Dunkerswell* [sic] *and Taunton Roads, all furnish delightful views. Although the town is quiet and modest, it is not behind the age, nor does it desire to waste its sweetness on the desert air. It has its golf links on the breezy downs seven hundred feet above the sea. It has its tennis club, its social clubs, and reading rooms. The old church ... reminds the visitor of the perfect repose of a country church and surrounding God's acre. For residents there is much in the town to make life agreeable. Unfortunately, houses are difficult to get, but this is surely a want which the enterprising citizens will supply. The ancient Grammar School of Allhallows gives a thoroughly good classical or modern education. There are also very good*

private schools for girls and young boys. For the sportsman, the Otter provides good trout fishing and tickets can be obtained from several farmers at moderate cost. True to its name, the Otter provides otters as well as trout ... Honiton is not likely to lose its old-world charm and rural beauty, and it is ready to welcome to its repose the discerning and appreciative visitor."

The ancient town of Honiton, because of its position on the main road from Exeter to London, has always been known to people travelling through the region. In the past many wayfarers stopped awhile to enjoy the hospitality of the town's numerous inns. One of the first public conveyances to pass through was in 1766. It carried just six passengers whose journey to London spanned two days – so much for eighteenth century 'Away Days' to the Capital! In 1789 the 'inside' fare to London was £2.12s.6d (£2.62) but if you were of limited means, or if you loved the 'great outdoors', then it was about two thirds of this to travel on top. In addition to this outlay passengers had to buy their own meals at inn stops along the way. Working class folk didn't travel far!

Through the first half of the nineteenth century roads and journey times improved greatly and by 1836 those travelling on the 'mail coach' could leave London at about 8.00 p.m. and be in Honiton, some 154 miles down the wibbly-wobbly way, by 11.00 a.m. the next day. This gave an average speed of just a shade more than an impressive ten miles per hour. Those without the necessary means keen to reach the capital often walked (and without being sponsored!), most taking more than a week to get there. However the railways were

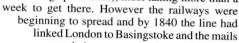

beginning to spread and by 1840 the line had linked London to Basingstoke and the mails were being conveyed more quickly. More importantly the days of the stage coach, and to some extent the coaching inn, were numbered. Farquharson's *History of Honiton* accounts for the demise of some of those inns. Some adapted and changed function: the Golden Lion was let out as rooms; the George became the 'redoubtable' Miss Fowler's shop; the Bell, the Cock, the Head and Horns, the Red Lion and the Red Hart all became domestic residences. Some were included on a roll of shame. Both the King's Head and the Oxford Inn, on opposite sides of the main street, and the Blue Ball were closed for being 'disorderly' houses, whilst the Black Horse and the Greyhound both had the misfortune to burn down.

In 1868 there were 24 surviving places of liquid refreshment. These were the Dolphin, Angel, White Hart, White Horse, White Lion, Black Lion, Red Cow, Lamb, Swan, Chopping Knife, London Inn, Exeter Inn, Three Tuns, Globe, Vine, King's Arms, Fountain, Crown & Sceptre, Anchor, Star, New Inn, Turk's Head, Volunteer Inn and, to mark the shape of things to come, the Railway Inn.

The line of the London and South Western Railway reached the town in 1860 and the town had 'a first-class station'. The engineer was Mr J. Locke, MP for the borough. His task of bringing the railway to the town was far from easy. A tunnel, a mile or so out of town, had to be cut through a high hill. The geology of the situation presented him with major problems, underground water appearing to play havoc with exposed layers of rock and large amounts of greensand being washed out of the tunnel sides. However it was the landlord of the Railway Inn who saved the day. He, like so many of his ilk, had other 'strings to his bow'. He was a builder and knew how best to arrest the constant subsidences which were occurring. He managed to make a rock restraint by using a mixture of timber and scrap iron which effectively cured the problem and made him a tidy sum of money.

The railway still runs through Honiton and to me, an Exonian, it's 'the Waterloo line', the slower way to London from the county town. The station has changed its appearance over the years as these two drawings, from a similar spot, demonstrate.

The Railway Inn, in Honiton's Queen Street, has had something of a chequered career and has changed names a few times. However, after being the 'Lazy Landlord' for a while, from 1977, it is now happily back on the right track again as the Railway Inn.

The former Volunteer Inn, at 177 High Street, has likewise seen a change of identity and is now the Pig & Barrow. Its sign reveals a merry-looking pig sat, not unsurprisingly, in a barrow. The background scenery shows some very pointy Alp-like mountains, not the sort usually found in East Devon. In the past this, one of the oldest such establishments in the town, has had a veritable procession of publicans and one of them, a man called Watts, used his horse and cart to run a delivery business from here. 'Diversification' is not a new concept!

Honiton's police station is a stone's throw from it and is a larger building than its predecessor which stood, more or less, on the same site. It originally had *"apartments for resident officers and also a magistrates' meeting room and 3 cells"*. When the new police station was constructed a shop and two small cottages were demolished.

Just below the police station is a small stream which has arrested the attention of locals at times. The Gissage (Giseage), a small river of about two to three miles in length, has played a watery part in the life of the lower part of the town. Farquharson wrote: *"The only other stream in the parish is the Giseage, and it takes its name from the fact of its source being the Gitt's hedge, the boundary between Gittisham and Honiton; this brook flows into the Otter at Stoney Bridge."* The river is bridged in various places and here are some extracts taken from an edition of the *Devon & Exeter Gazette* from 25 August 1925.

"The members of the Honiton Town Council, as well as the townspeople generally, are justly proud of the newly-erected Littletown Bridge over the River Gissage to carry what is known as Brickyard-road, an increasingly important thoroughfare leading from the main Honiton–Exeter road ... and thus tending to ease the traffic through the main street of the town. The new bridge, a reinforced concrete structure, takes the place of an old one that was quickly becoming incapable of meeting the demands made upon it, and its provision synchronises with an increasing volume of traffic on a road that has been in existence since Roman times ...

The erection of the bridge took seven months – a commendably short time in view of a certain amount of interruption caused by bad weather. The new bridge was officially declared open yesterday afternoon by the Mayor of Honiton (Mr H. R. Harris) in the presence of members of the Council and

a large gathering of townspeople ... Preparatory to the opening ceremony, the bridge was enclosed by means of streamers of white ribbons placed across the road at each end, and flags were displayed on both sides." Following the various speeches Mrs Phillips drove the Mayor over the new bridge in the first car and Mr Fothergill's car immediately followed with borough officials on board for an exceedingly short token trip.

The Gissage, despite its lack of length, has a very steep profile and there have been times when thunderstorms, and accompanying cloudbursts, have turned this normally tame trickle into an awesome flood. Such was the occasion in 1807 when a weir at Littletown was washed away and carried downstream. The flood also swept away a small wooden footbridge, which it carried along in the torrent. At the bridge in the main street the debris could not pass through and thus accumulated to form a dam. The ponded-back waters soon flooded neighbouring gardens and houses and for a while there was mayhem. The release and relief was sudden for under the considerable pressure the town bridge gave way and the Gissage's load swept swiftly on like a tidal wave, or bore, to join the Otter in one mad dash. At times like this, in the past, the road, which was once the bed of the river from Littletown to the present High Street, would have been more suitable for white water rafts than other non-aquatic vehicles! The name of this road, 'Watery Lane', could hardly have been more appropriate. Perhaps the former Anchor Inn, which closed in 1913 and stood close to where the Gissage passed the High Street, was well named! Today the stream is largely canalised in order to keep it in check when it rises swiftly after heavy, prolonged rain.

The Black Lion gives its name to, yes you have guessed, the present Black Lion Court, a small shopping mall, which lies adjacent to the junction of New Street and High Street in the higher part of the town. One of its previous owners was Jimmy Ayres, who also ran a butcher's shop. Its last landlord was Norman Carling. Where the main entrance to the mall is found was the yard of the Exeter Inn, now 84 High Street, and there are those who firmly believe it would have been more accurate to have called the shopping precinct 'Exeter Inn Court'. The Exeter Inn, one of a great many in Devon to possess such a name, closed in 1965.

New Street, which runs at a right angle from the town's main thoroughfare, contains a variety of businesses. This drawing shows the delicatessen which was once owned by Lewis Pavey.

The Star in New Street, not to be confused with the former Star Inn in High Street, is one that survives. Some senior townsfolk recall those Second World War years when Land

Army girls were billeted next door to it. At that time what is now New Street's car park was an attractive walled garden owned by Webbers. They ran a horticultural business and had the necessary gardening expertise to create something which was regarded as 'a bit special' in those days.

There are quite a few older thatched properties in and around the town and one small terrace, opposite the library in New Street, includes the Tudor House,

Middle Thatch and Thatch End. However the latter isn't thatched any more, despite its name.

The Chopping Knife, which was also called the Rolling Pin & Chopping Knife, probably had its name 'cut' by popular local usage, Devonians being traditionally lazy with their speech and always quick to abbreviate wherever 'poss'. However the ultimate 'chop' came sometime in the 1880s. It eventually became 'The Honiton Lace Shop'.

Yet another pub to change name, and not surprisingly, was the 'Knacker's Hole', in Northcote Lane. It later became the Mermaid but was left high and dry when it closed in 1905.

The White Horse, near the corner of Silver Street, ceased to be an inn in 1937. As a place of refreshment it had a long history. George Humphreye, a former landlord, was the great-great-grandfather of one of Honiton's most famous sons, Ozias Humphry. The apparent inconsistent spelling of the surname is not unusual as it was common, in a more illiterate world, for names to corrupt, through generations, either by word of mouth or by writing. An 'e' or two didn't seem to matter too much.

Ozias Humphry, born in 1742, was the son of a mercer and wig-maker. He became a famous portrait and miniature painter and ascended to the position of Royal Academician and Sergeant Painter to George II.

William Salter, born 1804, was another Honiton-born artist and Royal Academician, and painter of high repute. He took six years to complete his masterpiece, featuring around 83 figures, of the Waterloo Banquet, which was housed at Apsley House. He was the son of the town crier. His early working life was spent in the much humbler surroundings of the workhouse, where he was the schoolmaster.

The Manor House, formerly an old coaching inn called the Golden Lion (which closed in 1851) and built on the same site as the former town house of the abbots of Dunkeswell, has an interesting and eventful history.

At midnight on 15 May 1790 a fire broke out in the stables of this inn, then owned by a widow, Mrs Mitchell. The stables were partly occupied by horses belonging to the King's 1st Dragoon Guards. The casualty list included one stallion, three travellers' horses, five soldiers' horses and seventeen post horses. The fire didn't catch the Golden Lion alight but spread to nearby houses, of which thirty-nine were destroyed.

Horatio Nelson once spent a night at the Golden Lion and performed a noble deed whilst in Honiton. One of his favourite men, Captain Blagdon Westcott, had been killed in the Battle of the Nile. Nelson invited Westcott's mother and sister to have breakfast with him. On hearing that she had not received a gold service medal, to which her son would have been entitled had he survived, he took a medal from his own coat and presented it to her in the hope that she would accept it even though it had been worn by him.

Another famous visitor, albeit a fleeting one, was Charles Dickens, who entered Honiton, in a hurry, on his way to Exeter. He was covering an election for his paper, the *Morning Chronicle*, and was keen to scoop the story

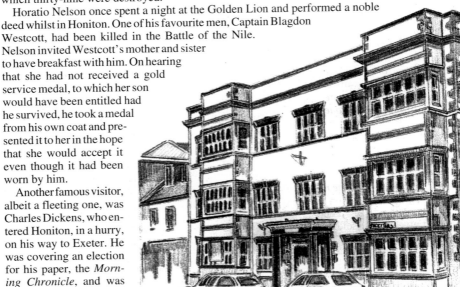

before his rival, Denison of *The Times*, could do so. The two, in their respective coaches, raced westwards. Dickens thought he had time to sample the fayre on offer at the Golden Lion and ordered a meal. Whilst it was being prepared Denison arrived! With no time to lose, and forsaking his meal, Dickens took flight and got to Exeter first.

The building has served other uses, having been a Post Office, headquarters for Honiton Rural District Council, home to the local branch of the Pearl Assurance Company and also a solicitors' office at one time.

This 'long-derelict Georgian building of architectural importance' made the headlines again in August 1976 when nine fire appliances raced to a fierce fire here. Three rooms on the first floor were destroyed whilst two thirds of the top floor and a quarter of the roof were gutted. Amazingly the exterior of the building remained largely intact and experts ruled that it didn't need to be shored up.

The firemen attending the blaze must have had a tough twenty-four hours, because previous to this blaze they fought a gorse fire near the Hare and Hounds on Gittisham Common and immediately after bringing the Golden Lion under control raced out to Brown Down, on the Blackdowns near Stopgate, to tackle another one.

The Manor House survived the blaze and major renovating works brought it back into full use in 1984, when several firms took the opportunity to move in, including the *Express and Echo* newspaper. Behind this fine building stood some twenty cottages, which were pulled down during the 1970s.

Farquharson's *History of Honiton* was published in 1868 by the Devon and Somerset Steam Printing Company of Waterbeer Street in Exeter. (This 'street of the water bearers' was partly demolished to make way for the Guildhall Shopping Centre but its route and several of its buildings are still there.) This now rare book was sold then as a crisp new publication by Miss Spurway, John Knight, and W. Clarke, stationers, in Honiton and all booksellers. It was dedicated by the author *"To his dear old friend, Miss Marsh, the oldest inhabitant of Honiton"*. This was the occasion of her 95th birthday and, no doubt, she would have been thrilled by such a gesture.

It tells us this, using pubs as guiding locational landmarks, about a fire in 1765: *"It commenced in a blacksmith's forge behind an inn named the Blacksmith's Arms, on the south side of the main street, a short distance to the east of the King's Arms Inn. The house directly opposite, on the north side of the High-street, was a thatched building occupied by a Mr Gibbons, a maltster, who had the previous day completed the thorough repair of his house and outbuildings. To prevent the sparks from the fire igniting his roof he covered it with pieces of wet serge, borrowed for the purpose off his friend, Mr Snook, a woollen manufacturer, but left the malthouse unprotected. The roof of this caught fire, and thus both sides of the street were in flames at one time."* The damage was extensive and there were some heart-rending scenes, which he graphically described, as the fire *"consumed 115 houses, extending on the south side of the town to the old Presbyterian chapel, which stood nearly opposite Clapper-lane, including the back street, to Honiton Great House, the residence of Mr Duke, MP., and now occupied by Messrs Ashley, tanners, the fire destroying, in its way, Allhallows Chapel, melting the bells in the tower, and a great portion of the charity property. This fire also burnt the houses that stood in the High-street, in the middle of the road, opposite Allhallows Chapel, and which faced towards the west. A Mr Darke, the schoolmaster of the Presbyterian chapel school, was burnt alive by this fire; he entered his house, then in flames, to recover some papers, and whilst there the roof fell in; after the event a hand and a piece of his arm were found grasping the latch of a door."*

The town has suffered other scares as well. Many years ago there was a firm which made gun cartridges, these being sold mainly to farmers. One day there was a mighty explosion and the roof of the premises was completely blown off, one man being injured in the process.

Today Honiton lacks a cinema and film-goers are obliged to go to Wellington, Taunton, Exeter or Sidmouth for their Big Screen entertainment. However in the past locals did not need to travel. In the 1920s they could visit Mr Harris's premises in High Street (overleaf) to see some amazing silent films. The upper room housed the projection equipment. As only one reel at a time could be set up to be shown, the projectionist, Albion Wyatt, often assisted by his son Jack, had to be a smooth operator when effecting the change-over whilst the often impatient audience awaited a restart of the action. There was a venting system for the projection equipment as it had a form of exhaust and if you look closely at the building today it can be spotted.

It was the custom in those days of yesteryear for pianists to watch the story unfold and accompany the action with appropriate music. Talented musicians could enhance a movie and make it seem more exciting than it probably was. However at this cinema the pianist was blind! Poor Tommy Vincent played beautifully but his music was often inappropriate to the story-line.

The cinema existed at a time when it was the norm for most people to smoke and as one can imagine the auditorium became a haze of thick bluish smoke. To help reduce the horrendous effects of a lethal cloud the cinema's commissionaire kept a 'Flit gun' which was employed during the interval but cinema-goers were divided in their opinion as to what was better, the smoke or the spray! Courting couples queued early for film shows because the back rows were double seats where it was possible for them to get closer to each other ...

The exits were located in the alley running down the side of it called 'Cinema Passage', now called St John's Close because when the cinema closed it became a St John ambulance depot. At the rear of this former place of entertainment was a row of cottages called Cinema Terrace.

The 'Devonia', which was built on the site of a pub called the Three Cups, was the town's cinema until 24 November 1962. On that fateful day, in the early hours of the morning, it was largely destroyed by yet another major fire which also threatened to spread to several other nearby properties, these including thatched cottages, on the north side of the High Street, many roofs having been set alight. The combined efforts of brigades from Colyton, Axminster, Ottery St Mary and Honiton itself soon brought it under control. Only the front of the cinema remained intact.

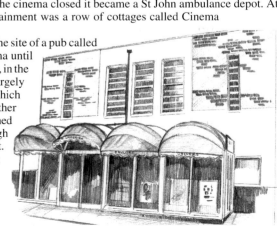

St Michael's church was the scene of yet another major fire in late March 1911. It was discovered by the sexton, who told his wife to save what she could before he ran down the steep Church Hill to tell church officials of the crisis. Word was spread around the town as fast as possible so that by 10.30 a.m., quite a time after the start of the fire, helpers and the fire brigade got to work on the building. Meanwhile the rector had contacted Exeter's fire brigade, who raced to the railway station in Queen Street (Exeter Central), where a special train waited to carry them, their steam engine and the four horses needed to pull it. Being so high above the town water was a problem. A ditch carrying a small watercourse was dammed so that some water could be extracted. The Exeter crew made use of a mill stream much lower down the hillside and with the use of almost 2000 feet of hose brought more water to the burning building. Eventually the fire was brought under control but much damage had been caused by the holocaust. However it was restored and a re-dedication ceremony, conducted by the Bishop of Exeter, followed in late August the following year.

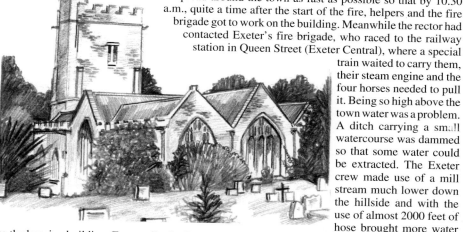

There was one tradition employed by funeral parties in the past. Mourners would agree to meet at the bottom of Church Hill. From here they proceeded up the steep hill to this church and whilst they made their way, rather than engage themselves in conversation, they would chant Psalm 144 until they reached the church.

This cemetery was the scene of a dispute, one which involved the law in July 1896. It appears that soil from beneath the church was used in repairing the nearby road, this deed leading to something of an 'unholy' row. The main complaints stemmed from the stench that came with it and the notion that a spring nearby was the source of a water supply for a farm and other properties on this hillside. What really upset a number of local people was that human bones, a jawbone with three teeth still intact and the handle of a coffin appeared in this soil. However when all the witnesses had been consulted the chairman of the magistrates said that he and his colleagues were of the unanimous opinion that the charges against the rector, the churchwardens and the contractor had not been sustained and the summonses were dismissed.

Rising by the church is Marlpits Hill, the scene, more than three centuries ago, of a tragic incident which translated into a ghostly sighting for a group of schoolchildren in 1904. They were walking here, with their teacher, when several of them looked distinctly off colour. When quizzed by their teacher they told of seeing a tall, wild-looking man who was coated in thick mud. He wore the sort of wide-brimmed hat that was more typical of the late seventeenth century.

This ghost was believed to be a survivor of the bloody battle, the last to be fought on English soil, at Sedgemoor in 1685 between the ill-fated followers of the Duke of Monmouth and royal troops. On that misty day there was wholesale carnage with over 300 more to follow later at the hands of Judge Jeffreys. (See also pages 28 and 29.)

'Our man' legged it away from the battlefield, crossing the flat Somerset countryside to reach the hills of Devon. Living rough, he had just made it back to his Honiton home on Marlpits Hill, his wife and child at the door to greet him, when supporters of the king arrived and cut him down as they watched in horror.

The crude cottage in which the poor man and his family lived has long since been demolished, and his spirit has not been seen in recent years. But according to the not-so-reassuring Archie Farquharson " ... *every dark lane has its ghost.*"

The apparently ghost-free Globe, in the High Street, may never have set the world alight itself but had its moments. It had traded under various names like the Compass before undergoing a change of direction to become the Carpenters Arms. Whatever its name it was a much more sociable building than the one previously on the same site, because this was a bridewell or prison. The pub enjoyed a decent trade from the Gloucester Regiment, stationed near the town, but when it was relocated to Germany, in 1971, the Globe's own world was shattered and it closed down. Next door to it, Raleigh House, in the past, was a boarding house, just one of many in the town.

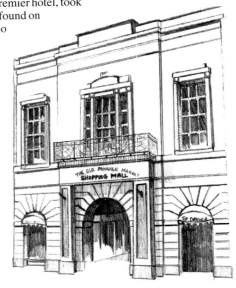

Two pubs to disappear in the 1970s were the Lamb and the Fountain, both Devenish brewery houses, the Weymouth-based firm shedding many inns across the region at that time.

The Fountain had been run by different members of the Cox family for 36 years and it was quite a shock for the family to see their livelihood suddenly disappear. A similar situation existed at the Lamb, where the Ackland family connection had gone back even further. They had taken over the pub's running in 1911 but Mr Ackland was killed in action during the First World War. His widow, Alice, assumed control and ran it for many years. Her son, Les, took it over in 1964 and had ten years as licensee until the pub's sudden closure, like the proverbial lamb led to the slaughter.

The Dolphin, always regarded as the town's premier hotel, took its name from the creature, a dolphin embowed, found on the family crest of the Courtenays, a family who have held the title of Earl of Devon for many centuries. It was probably a manor house of theirs, since they had enjoyed strong links with Honiton for hundreds of years. The hotel has endured fluctuating fortunes. In 1878 when William Henry Banfield was in charge its directory entry was *"Dolphin" Family and Commercial Hotel & Posting House.* He was also further listed under Dolphin Assembly Rooms, for entertainments and lectures. Mr Banfield ran his own horse-and-carriage conveyance business, which allowed him to offer visitors arriving by train a 'free ride' to the hotel. In later years William Norman was the driver but it's believed the horses, having made the journey so many times, intuitively knew their way so well that they could have done it without him. Fortunately this theory was never put to the test!

14

This inn had a string of owners and some made their mark more than others. Mr Fitch was responsible for building its beautiful ballroom, in about 1923, which had eight bedrooms above it. Alas this fine dance hall was sacrificed by a developer who saw a better return by converting it to more bedrooms. At one time the premises next door were a Woolworth shop.

The Dolphin now has the name 'New' in front of it and much has been done in recent years to return it to the high standard of accommodation that it was in the past.

Dolphin Court, a small shopping precinct, one of several in Honiton, is reached by an arch beside the New Dolphin Hotel. Nearby is the Old Pannier Market with not a pannier in sight these days! Here there was once a Saturday market where the fresh merchandise, carried to town in panniers strung across the backs of beasts of burden, was sold. For a while a steam-driven fire engine was housed here. At Carnival time, in the past (and Honiton is famous for its fine carnivals!) this venue was turned into a skittle alley.

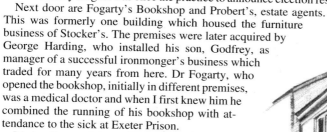

During the Second World War the needy came here to receive bread and soup. It appears there was once a fine banqueting room upstairs, now fronted by a balcony. From this lofty ledge it was once the practice to announce election results.

Next door are Fogarty's Bookshop and Probert's, estate agents. This was formerly one building which housed the furniture business of Stocker's. The premises were later acquired by George Harding, who installed his son, Godfrey, as manager of a successful ironmonger's business which traded for many years from here. Dr Fogarty, who opened the bookshop, initially in different premises, was a medical doctor and when I first knew him he combined the running of his bookshop with attendance to the sick at Exeter Prison.

It's hardly surprising to hear that when some of Honiton's older properties undergo renovation various finds occur. In 1973 when the King's Arms was being altered the landlord, Reg Sherlock, discovered a magic lantern bricked up in the walls. With this was 'a peep show', one of naughty Victorian pictures, tame by today's standards, probably wickedly wonderful by theirs.

The Red Cow, further along the High Street, was, in the nineteenth century, a place of great revelry and, occasionally, one where the customers became animated and boisterous, the demon drink being the fuel for fights and fisticuffs. The pub had, like the Fountain, a bit of a reputation as a drinking house for gypsies, and at the time of the Fair 'feathers were ruffled' and the ensuing fights spilled over into the street.

A policeman called Dicky Morcambe perfected his own way of dealing with those who brawled in public. He had hands 'as big as hams' and used them to good purpose, 'apprehending' one troublemaker with each of them. Using his terrific strength he would then bang their heads together, thereby dramatically and speedily ending the dispute. Fighting gypsies, of those pre-paracetamol days, soon realised that this was a painful solution and whenever Morcambe appeared on the scene they became wise and parted like the waters of the Red Sea!

Originally the pub had an arch at one side, which horses being led to stables at the rear passed through. In the nineteenth century the pub was much smaller but to make it a more viable concern it was later enlarged, at the expense of two adjacent cottages.

The Fountain, at the other end of the town, held an extra advantage for gypsies (and other pony dealers) because outside were, and still are,

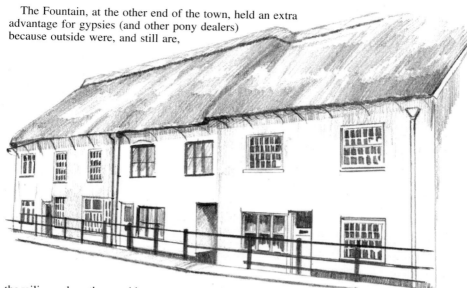

the railings where they could tie up the horses which they brought to town to sell or trade.

The Carlton Inn owed its early success to a healthy charabanc trade. There was a procession of coaches calling in here for their passengers to get refreshment. Not too many locals patronised this 'watering-hole' so they were not too aggrieved when the owner moved to more suitable premises on the outskirts of town. The newly-built Turk's Head roadhouse was designed to handle even

greater numbers of charabancs and customers. For a long while it was a restaurant and function room but after having a relatively quick turnover of different owners it was bought by Slade's in 1983. They moved out of the town centre to become firmly established there as 'Slade's Countrywise', the larger Turks Head building ideal for expansion.

Slade's started principally by supplying feedstuffs, mostly to the farm trade, in the end part of the Pannier Market building. However having first moved, in 1952, along the road, the firm saw the opportunities which their present site offered.

The Honiton town centre skyline is dominated by the 104-foot high tower of the slightly set-back

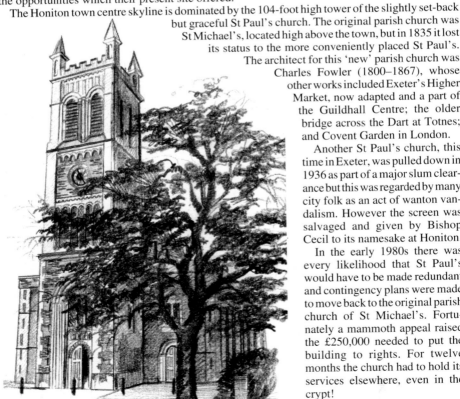

but graceful St Paul's church. The original parish church was St Michael's, located high above the town, but in 1835 it lost its status to the more conveniently placed St Paul's. The architect for this 'new' parish church was Charles Fowler (1800–1867), whose other works included Exeter's Higher Market, now adapted and a part of the Guildhall Centre; the older bridge across the Dart at Totnes; and Covent Garden in London.

Another St Paul's church, this time in Exeter, was pulled down in 1936 as part of a major slum clearance but this was regarded by many city folk as an act of wanton vandalism. However the screen was salvaged and given by Bishop Cecil to its namesake at Honiton.

In the early 1980s there was every likelihood that St Paul's would have to be made redundant and contingency plans were made to move back to the original parish church of St Michael's. Fortunately a mammoth appeal raised the £250,000 needed to put the building to rights. For twelve months the church had to hold its services elsewhere, even in the crypt!

Honiton Past and Present

The church's clock was the work of Matthew Murch of Honiton. In the 1930s there were complaints about the unharmonious chimes waking guests at the almost adjacent Angel Hotel. Mr J. J. Hall wrote to the local newspaper about the chimes: *"To begin with, I think that Mr Sprake, who was a local councillor, for St Paul's Ward, and his patrons, those who frequent his hotel, have a real grievance. There are chimes and there are c-h-i-m-e-s ... apart from their very close proximity, the bells now under consideration are anything but pleasing to the musical ear, and certainly do no credit to such a remarkably fine thoroughfare as the High St of Honiton."* It was mooted that an inexpensive device could be fitted to stop the bells chiming between midnight and six a.m. as had been done at Okehampton and Bridport.

A referendum was held which was couched as follows: *"Are you in favour of stopping the chimes of the Town Clock between the hours of midnight and 6 a m?"* Ratepayers were entitled to vote. Out of a possible 953 votes, 779 exercised the right to record an opinion. Of these 456 wanted to silence the night-time chimes whilst 323, probably those oblivious to them or out of immediate earshot, wanted them to continue.

The Angel was once a thriving hostelry. It survived a serious fire in 1765 and in the mid-nineteenth century was modernised. An extra storey was added to create more room. The pub had various owners and landlords. One of them was the aforementioned Ralph Sprake, who diversified by also running a taxi service and had a garage and motor repair shop in the hotel's yard. He was also the captain of the local fire brigade and it was a common sight to see the fire engine in the yard. At one time the Inland Revenue Office was based at the hotel, with Mr J. L. Murch playing the role of 'villain of the piece' as the dreaded tax collector. However times have changed and the Angel became a fallen one when it ceased being a pub in 1989 to become apartments. The ground floor is now an off licence so perhaps it has remained in high spirits after all.

Following its closure there was a mammoth auction in late November that year and many took advantage of it to buy both bargains and keepsakes of an inn which had survived fires but could not weather an economic crisis.

Close by is the Mackarness Hall, where I have given a number of talks over the years. It is named after a former rector of Honiton, John Fielder Mackarness (1855–1870), who married the daughter of Sir John Taylor Coleridge and went on from here to become Bishop of Oxford. Typical of the Rev Mackarness's efforts was the holding of church services for 'navvies' working on the railroad. These services he held in a humble carpenters' hut close to the tunnel, mentioned earlier, towards Axminster.

The well-known Allhallows School at Rousdon, between Colyford and Lyme Regis, from 1938 onwards, sadly, for economic reasons,

closed at Christmas 1998. It originated at Honiton in buildings in, around and close to St Paul's church. It survived an earlier crisis in Victorian times when the Rev Mackarness doubled up his duties as priest and headmaster.

The school's former chapel had one of its several 'facelifts' in 1903 when it was lovingly restored to a place of worship as a memorial to those who fell in the South African War. It is believed to have served as a schoolroom and dining hall for some three centuries, but it is now, with so many fine exhibits, Honiton Museum, a place well worth visiting. Here you will learn a great deal more about this East Devon town's past. The Museum has been advertised as having 'The best collection of Honiton Lace in the world' but it has many other diversions to interest and educate. Rather than letting me give away too many of its secrets, why not make a visit?

Many of the chapel's chattels and fittings were removed to Rousdon. When Allhallows School was still in Honiton the headmaster lived almost on top of his work in 'Junior House', this being the tall building now occupied by Stag's. They took it on from auctioneers T. D. Hussey & Son, a firm established in 1777 who once conducted business for the sale of livestock and produce at Honiton Market. It was common to see the wide main street filled with cattle. On market days residents and shop owners kept their front doors shut because it was not unusual for animals to panic and bolt. Imagine the damage which could be done by an errant cow in your parlour! Horses were sold at one end of the High Street whilst cattle and sheep changed hands at the other.

An annual ceremony which takes place during the town's fair is mentioned in Arthur Mee's *Devon* (1938): *"Then from the window of an inn* [the King's Arms] *handfuls of hot pennies are thrown into the street and children burn their fingers with them and cool them in the stream which is conveniently running for them by the kerb. This little runnel was called 'The Lakes' and started in a spring called 'The Fountain'."* Or as Farquharson put it: *"Throughout the whole length of both the principal streets, runs a stream of clear water, with occasional dipping places, adding much to the cleanliness and comfort of the inhabitants'."* The waters here were also noted,

not for the healing of burnt fingers but for the curing of eye disorders. However at times this reputation was abused when it was the practice to turn some unfortunates upside down and dunk them in the deeper pools found in this watercourse.

The *Western Morning News* report of 1953 said this: *"Surrounded by a crowd of excited children and holidaymakers, Honiton's town crier, Mr J. Lake, yesterday opened the town's historic fair which will reach its 700th anniversary in four years time. Mr Lake, wearing a striking uniform of gold and blue and a three-cornered hat, came out from the Pannier Market at noon carrying a garlanded pole surmounted by a golden glove, and cried the following proclamation which used to apply to debtors: 'Oyez! Oyez! The glove is up. The fair has begun. No man shall be arrested until the glove is taken down. God save the Queen.'*

The words were repeated by the crowd three times, who then followed Mr Lake to the Angel Hotel, where the proprietors, Mr and Mrs R. D. Sprake, and their guests, threw hot pennies into the street. Children and some adults scrambled for them.

Then on to the King's Arms Hotel, where the pole and the glove were placed on the balcony. It will remain there until tomorrow, when Mr Lake will carry it to the White Lion at the other end of the town.

At the King's Arms the proclamation was cried again and the Mayor and Mayoress of Honiton (Mr and Mrs R. J. Cann) threw hot pennies into the street."

But colourful though it is, the present-day Honiton Fair is only a shadow of its former self. Older residents recall when the Fair included roundabouts and cages of lions.

One of Honiton's oldest grocers, Mr G. Bassett, recalled that this was the day farmers paid their yearly bills. To welcome them, tradesmen provided meals and drinks. The farmer and his family could go to one establishment for lunch, to another for tea and quench their thirsts at a third. He added: *"The High St was packed with stalls and sideshows, including a troupe of dancing girls. At the other end of the town horses were bought and sold. And at the fair farm labourers changed maisters."*

Dimond's, stationers and booksellers, are located at 74 High Street. If you look at their trade name or their letterheads, you will notice that the 'A' of A. Dimond & Son is a big one. Recent generations of the Dimond family have deliberately chosen this letter for family members' Christian names. Arthur, who succeeded Archie, passed the business on to his son Antony, and his children have names all beginning with an A. Their firm is the oldest surviving family business trading in the town. In 1988 they celebrated their centenary, the business having been started by Robert and Eliza Dimond in 1888.

No 70 High Street, just a few doors along the road from A. Dimond, was described as an 'eyesore' when it was auctioned in the mid 1970s for a knock-down price. This was a working men's club at one time. During the Great War it was used as a hospital and for many years the curate of St Paul's lived on its first floor. Its other uses include that of being the Toc H club and a Post Office social club.

There are many churches of other denominations in Honiton. The Baptist church, next to the Manor House, serves a very different function to the building which previously stood on its site. This was the Swan Inn which, not surprisingly, bearing in mind the town's somewhat heated history, was burnt down in 1840. Following the disaster the pub was relocated on the opposite side of the road but closed almost exactly half a century later and is now a private house. The only reminder of its existence is that the original stable yard is still called 'Swan Yard'.

In 1981 there was controversy when a pair of commemorative gates were removed from the Baptist church so that a wider access could be created. These had

been placed to the memory of three former worshippers, F. J. Matthews, R. Smith and F. White, at a special dedication ceremony on 20 November 1949. The plaque giving details was saved and relocated but the gates were sold off for an undisclosed amount ...

The Methodist church was in New Street but later became the meeting place for both senior citizens and the local town council, not necessarily one and the same thing! To continue their worship the Methodists moved to premises literally 'just around the corner' in the aptly-named Chapel Street, a stone's throw from their earlier home. They are now handily placed next door to the Honiton DIY centre.

Honiton, as we have seen, has one of the longest, straightest and widest main streets, for a town of its size, in England. People old enough to remember the days before the Honiton bypass, opened in 1966 by Minister of Transport Barbara Castle, will recall just how long it took to pass from one end of the town to the other on summer Saturdays.

The one day when no traffic passed through this busy thoroughfare was the occasion of Queen Elizabeth II's Silver Jubilee celebrations which took place on a 'joyous' summer's day in June 1977. The bells of St Paul's rang out and some 1500 lucky schoolchildren were each presented with a commemorative mug. Doing the honours were the Mayor and Mayoress (Mr and Mrs Alun Thomas), their deputies (Mr and Mrs Patrick Allen), the Jubilee Committee Chairman and his wife (Mr and Mrs Ron Gigg) and a former Alderman, Mr F. W. C. Tucker. At that time he was one of just two living freemen of the borough. A celebration tea was arranged for pensioners in New Street and there were also sports and dances to complete a memorable day for many of the townsfolk.

Another occasion when there was no motor traffic in the town centre, but for the more obvious reason that there wasn't any in those days, was the celebration of the coronation of Queen Victoria in 1838. Business was suspended, and all work brought to a standstill for the day. The procession, headed by a band, was a grand one. *"There were the schoolchildren, made up by 'a School of Industry' and National and Sunday Schools; the ladies, two and two; lacemakers with garlands; Female Club also with garlands. Then another band followed by the clergy 'in full canonicals'; constables with staves; the bailiff with his mace; the Portreeve; the Aletasters; members of the Friendly Societies in their regalias in the following order, the Old Friendly Society, the New Friendly Society, the Third Friendly Society and the New United Brethren Society; followed in the rear by traders, sporting bright colours, including the coachmakers, the wheelwrights, the smiths, the cordwainers and the tailors and 'the gentlemen and inhabitants of the town three and three.' A pretty sight they made as they passed with measured steps and stateliness under the laurel arches which adorned the streets.*

Among the general celebrations were the regaling of people with roast beef and plum pudding and a public dinner at the Golden Lion Inn for the gentlemen of the neighbourhood."

Going back even further, when the Napoleonic Wars ended the townspeople of a thriving Honiton decided to organise a carnival of celebrations as a form of thanksgiving. They invited people from all over East Devon to participate. Beer and Seaton sent 'a cart load of smugglers' and

Branscombe sent 'a donkey chaise full of lace makers'. The best contribution came from Colyton, where they harnessed the first wagon ever built in that town, a beautiful blue and scarlet contraption, which was filled with the local band. Hundreds descended on Honiton for a grand ball where the Colyton bandsmen entertained. The beat to the music was tapped out in a highly original way by Sebastian Isaac, a trader who used his wooden leg to keep time. He beat it with such enthusiasm that it almost fell off!

The architecture and dates of the town's buildings have been largely dictated by some destructive fires which have gutted many buildings in the long main street at various times. Nevertheless some of the ones which have replaced them have been appreciated. In his *Devon Survey* (1932) W. Harding Thompson had this to say: *"... Of the towns in the valley, Honiton is probably the most distinguished in East Devon: it lies astride the Exeter–London road, and thus, ever since the establishment of the stage coach, it has been an important halting place for travellers to the west. There are few towns which express their character so well in the street architecture; the wide main street, bordered by channels of running water, has several Georgian houses and shop fronts of fine proportion and refined detail: these should be preserved as long as possible, for these are as much an asset to the borough as the famous lace industry ..."*

Honiton has had its industries and some of them are famous worldwide!

In a Devonshire word association game certain places beg to be matched like Widecombe (Fair), Devonshire (cream or dumplings), Dartmoor (ponies or prison), Dartington (glass), Tavistock (Goosie Fair) and Honiton, of course, is always synonymous with lace.

This was written about lace-making in 1888, a time when the industry was well past its peak: *"Honiton lace has had a curious history with many fluctuations. It is said to have been first introduced by the Flemings, who took refuge in England to escape the persecutions of the Duke of Alva. Many Flemish names are still to be found in the neighbourhood of Honiton – namely Stocker, Murch, Trump, &c.*

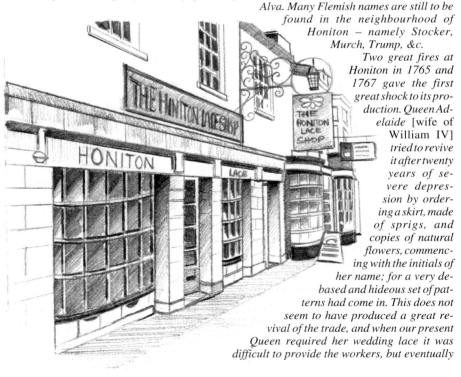

Two great fires at Honiton in 1765 and 1767 gave the first great shock to its production. Queen Adelaide [wife of William IV] *tried to revive it after twenty years of severe depression by ordering a skirt, made of sprigs, and copies of natural flowers, commencing with the initials of her name; for a very debased and hideous set of patterns had come in. This does not seem to have produced a great revival of the trade, and when our present Queen required her wedding lace it was difficult to provide the workers, but eventually*

a dress worth £1,000 was made at the small fishing village of Beer. The English Royal Family have been the most constant patrons of Honiton lace, and have done immense good in keeping the trade alive."

At the end of the seventeenth century almost 5000 people derived their livelihoods from this industry and more than a quarter of them were based in Honiton, the heartland of lace and so much a focal point of activities that the town's name was attached to it.

However despite the overall decline in the fortunes of the Honiton lace industry there was still a demand and Mrs Fowler set up a successful business with her Honiton Lace Shop. Her obituary, albeit a short one, appeared in the *Devon & Exeter Gazette* on 16 December 1929: *"The death has occurred of Mrs A. Fowler at the age of 90, one of the oldest inhabitants of Honiton. She was the founder of the Honiton Lace Shop, and did much to revive the industry. The deceased was the holder of many Royal warrants, having been honoured with commissions from the English and Foreign Royal families."* Her entry in the *Devonshire Directory* for 1878 stated: *"Mrs W. Fowler (late Ward), Honiton lace manufacturer, patronized by Her Majesty the Queen and HRH Princess Louise, Marchioness of Lorne, High street."*

This drawing shows Mrs Elizabeth Cotty, who also had the honour of making lace for Royalty in the persons of three queens, Queen Victoria, Queen Alexandra and Queen Mary.

The Honiton Lace Shop contains some wonderful examples of the art and the importance of the lace industry is also acknowledged in the name of a new shopping precinct, Lace Walk, which joins the High Street to one of the town's biggest car parks. There are also mosaics on the wall of a supermarket to illustrate not only the lace industry but also other activities like the pottery industry and weaving. The Mickelburgh Foundry also has a panel and those observant visitors who pass along this pedestrian corridor to or from the car park are treated to a Honiton history lesson.

Looking through the business section of a modern telephone directory for East Devon under the 'Honiton' listing reveals that the only 'Honiton' recorded which is not in Honiton itself is a pub, the Honiton Inn, in Paris Street, Exeter, where the pub's sign depicts Honiton lace!

The town's woollen trade flourished in the seventeenth and eighteenth centuries. At one time the manufacture of serges employed over a thousand of the townsfolk but the decline of the industry occurred when industries polarised and developed in the North of England.

It is known that there was a pottery industry in the town as long ago as 1643 but the early wares produced were of primitive brown earthenware. It was not until the late nineteenth century that a potter called James Webber began to create more worthy pottery. His baking dishes, flower pots and bread pans found a ready market in Exeter, some 17 miles away, but only after James had endured a tough day's 'marketing' of his wares. He would set out at an unearthly hour and return in the early hours of the following day. He probably had little idea of how his work in the production of brown earthenware would be continued and later developed into such a flourishing industry in the twentieth century. Mr Collard ran the business from 1918 and found an international market for his products in a great number of countries around the globe. Until 1947 the raw material of clay was excavated from a point behind the pottery and then processed ready to be used for pottery manufacture. This was replaced by a specially prepared white clay.

Perhaps this history of producing quality goods is, in part, responsible for the town now being a leading antiques centre, with numerous shops selling a wide range of unusual and valuable items. The range of goods found in the town is incredible and draws devotees of the exotic from far afield in the hope of a 'bargain' or something quite rare and beautiful. 'Yellow Pages' included more than twenty listings for Honiton at the time when this book was researched

and as many of these contain more than one dealer there are probably more than double this number trading in the town. Between them they cover almost every type of article imaginable. For a town of its modest size this is quite an incredible situation, Honiton must surely be the antiques capital of the region.

The Honiton Antique Centre was once the YMCA; there are many 'senior' Honitonians who recall the fond days of their misspent youth spent playing snooker or table tennis here. An old chap called Hatherly, who sported a hat and smoked a pipe whilst sat in a comfortable chair, ran the place. When the building was sold the YMCA maintained their presence in the town by occupying premises at the rear of their former centre.

Honiton draws its shoppers, if not its drinkers, from a wide area and its unique charms attract holidaymakers. A number of family-run specialist shops enjoy good trade because many come to the town to escape the run-of-the-mill massive chain stores which dominate the centres of large towns and cities. The thrill for the new shoppers of Honiton is that they are never quite sure what's going to turn up. The overall impression conveyed is of a bustling, busy, thriving and generally prosperous place.

Almost all of the businesses to trade in Honiton's main shopping streets have changed hands down the years. Mr F. D. Stocker had premises a 'few doors down' from the Angel, in the first part of the twentieth century. In the 1930 *Devonshire Directory* an entry lists 'Stocker Fras D. jun cabinet maker High st'. Mr F. D. Stocker owned land which was sold off. His field became Langford Avenue, which lies behind Marwood House.

Marwood House, the oldest in the town, now the home of Roderick P. Butler, a well-known antique dealer, is where Charles II supposedly stayed a few times when in this area. The house is named after Thomas Marwood, who was physician to Queen Elizabeth I, but was built by his second son, John, in 1619, two years after his father's death. It was restored in 1828 and modernised in 1930. A cork tree, believed to have been planted by Sir Walter Raleigh, once stood in the garden but was blown down in a gale.

Thomas Marwood, at the age of 81, was famous for having cured the Earl of Essex's foot when all the other top doctors of the day had failed to stem the disease in it. And what is more amazing is the fact that a man with so obvious a propensity for healing the sick should secure long life for himself. When Thomas was a mere lad of 87 he took his second wife, Christine Serle, and defied the logical pattern of things by outliving her to marry, yet again, at the more mature age of 94. His bride this time around was Temperance Thatcher and, far from her finishing him off, he enjoyed a new lease of life and lived on for another eleven years, finally 'popping his (well-worn) clogs' at the grand old age of 105. Beyond his death he showed, as a benefactor, his love of Honiton and its people with a number of bequests.

A drinking fountain in New Street was dedicated to the memory of another Honiton medical man. This time the surgeon Mr Samuel Devenish, who was the Mayor of Honiton in 1856, was acknowledged. He passed away about three years later, on 5 February 1859.

There are, however, no memorials to another surgeon, a brave 20-year-old called Potts. He had joined the cause of the Duke of Monmouth in that fateful year of 1685 and was, no doubt, a participant in the last battle on English soil at Sedgmoor in Somerset. The Duke's supporters fled, if they could, but many were apprehended and tried by the infamous Judge Jeffreys. Four of them, along with young Potts, 'met their Maker' when they were publicly executed near St Margaret's Chapel.

The town's Market House, according to the *Devonshire Directory* of 1930, was built in about 1820 *"by the Paving Trust Commissioners, at a cost above £2,000. The market is held on Saturdays and is well supplied with cattle and all sorts of provisions; and great quantities of butter are sent weekly to London."*

At the western end of Honiton are the thatched St Margaret's almshouses complete with a chapel (32 feet x 13 feet) which was once a leper hospital. Although it was mentioned in documents in 1374 the current building was rebuilt by its second founder, Awliscombe-born Thomas Chard, the last abbot of Ford (1520–1539), an abbey on the Devon border with Somerset. *"The hospital consisteth*

of an house with five apartments, one for the Governor and four for leprous people, with a handsome chapel annexed for God's service." Here it is shown in two drawings, one based on how it was perceived in 1792, with artistic licence, and the other as it appeared recently.

However this part of the town has not always been at peace. In 1586 the Devon Lent Assizes were shifted to Honiton because the plague was raging in Exeter. Two judges, Sir Edmund Anderson, and Mr Baron Gent, presided over the proceedings and as a consequence of their judgements some 17 criminals were executed and buried close to the chapel.

It was believed that at a site nearby the dreadful Judge Jeffreys killed several followers of the Duke of Monmouth by boiling them in pitch. Following this horrendous deed their disembowelled limbs were exhibited at the former Shambles in the High Street.

The wartime barracks of Heathfield Camp (sited on land of the former Heathfield Farm), which was nearby, itself disappeared under heavy redevelopment in the 1990s. My first memories of it date back to the early 1950s when I was just a child passenger on a Slater's fruit and vegetable lorry from Exeter which delivered there each week. To one so young and so small it seemed a big camp and in the Second World War, then not that long finished, it was a busy place. Here many Americans were based, the black troops segregated from the white.

The camp saw many pass through: various regiments; Ugandan Asians thrown out by Idi Amin; film makers; and in its last years the homeless, who were accommodated in conditions which they were, for the most part, unhappy about, if the number of press reports are to be believed.

In the summer of 1978 BBC2 commissioned a programme called *The Vanishing Army*, about a sergeant-major trying to come to terms with civilian life after several tours of duty in Northern Ireland. It starred Bill Paterson, who went on to become the shady character Ally Fraser in the cult television series *Auf Wiedersehen Pet* during the 1980s. The local fire brigade were pressed into action, turning a fine day into a wet one by setting their water jets over the set. About 50 extras were taken on, these having been weeded out from a list of some 500 hopefuls. The pay was £12 a day, which included free meals, and the briefest of auditions were held at the New Dolphin Hotel. Other locations used included Gittisham Hill House and the snooker room of the local Conservative club. It was screened on 27 November 1978, several familiar Honiton faces being recognised in this *Play for Today* production.

The camp was demolished in 1988.

As we have seen, Honiton was an important coaching town but the roads in the district, although following a similar pattern, have changed their routes over the years. Farquharson, in about 1868, had this to say: "*All the roads, or nearly so, approaching the town are modern. The way to Axminster, known as the New road, was formed from a narrow lane called Shipley lane, that ran from Copper Castle gate to the entrance of Hale lane, the space between that part and Marwood House being a field called Shipley Close. Hale lane continued into the Taunton road but this portion was closed on the formation of the new road; at the first gate leading to Hale farm formerly stood a turnpike.*"

The old Axminster road ran under Springfield and over Mount Pleasant, and not as it now runs by the New Inn.

The old British Highway passed in front of St Michael's church, and continues by the Turks' Head Inn to Hembury Fort, using, for a short portion of the distance, the bed of the Giseage, which part is called Watery lane. Another portion of this stream was formerly a road leading from Hind street to the Manor. The old road to Taunton from Honiton was through Combe Raleigh and Luppitt."

The 1903 OS map shows the road to Axminster, towards the top of the hill, as 'King's Road'. Various wayfarers travelled these highways before they were up to much. It was on the road in from Chard that Daniel Defoe (1660–1731) (he of *Robinson Crusoe* fame) first cast eyes on the Otter valley and described it as *"the most beautiful landscape in the world ... "* He was also most complimentary about Honiton, saying that it was *"a large and beautiful market town, very populous and well built."*

The crenellated Copper Castle sits on the lofty slopes above the town on the A35 road to Axminster. It has an unusual design for a tollhouse and it's also rare that it still possesses its gates.

These are now set back from the road and no longer restrain or delay traffic. No doubt doctors

and vicars, on foot, would have approached this tollhouse with a more relaxed air for they didn't have to dig deep into their pockets to find the penny toll required to proceed on through this turnpike gate. But such exemptions were rare and the day the road became 'free' there was much celebrating.

In 1789 a crowd gathered here to greet George III, who paid an official visit to the town whilst travelling from Weymouth, where there is a fine statue of him near the sea front, to Plymouth. It's interesting to see that he chose the hazardous road journey along tracks we would consider to be primitive rather than sail down the Channel. All the young ladies, some 350 in number, dressed uniformly, their clothing adorned with white ribbons.

The *Devon & Exeter Gazette* reported on a gun which was formerly sited at Copper Castle but one should hasten to add that this wasn't stationed there to be used on toll-dodgers! However it became such an eyesore that Honiton Town Council, in late August 1929, decided to do something about it. Under the heading *"Monstrosity"* the report of their meeting said this: *"Honiton Town Council unanimously decided last evening to remove the gun which has for some years occupied a position by the roadside at Copper Castle. The matter arose on a letter from Dr D. Steele-Perkins, which the Town Clerk (Mr C. N. Tweed) read as follows 'May I, as a ratepayer, suggest to the council that it is time that awful monstrosity of the war ... be disposed of. It is at present an eyesore* to the most beautiful entrance to the town, being covered in rust. And I am quite sure none of us wants to be reminded any more of the awful times we went through, especially those who lost relatives in the war. Perhaps you will lay the matter before your Council, who, no doubt, will take what action they consider advisable."

The Mayoress (Mrs E. W. Matthews) agreed with the letter: *"I don't know how the gun came here. I suppose it was given us as a trophy of the war by the English. Could not the Council write to the War Office and ask if it would like the gun back again? It is generally felt that everyone has suffered enough as a result of the war and we do not want to have something to remind them of it. Possibly the gun could be hidden in the stinging nettles at Shipley Close.'* She moved that it be removed. Mr Studley seconded. Mr Maers considered that the gun which, he said, was given to the town in connection with the War Savings movement should be sold or scrapped. The Town Clerk said that he should like to refer to the correspondence that took place at the time before the council came to any decision to sell the gun. It might be necessary to get the sanction of the War Office if a sell was proposed. It was unanimously decided that the gun be moved, the question of its future being referred to the General Purposes Committee with power to act."

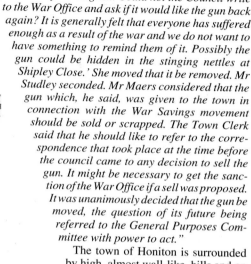

The town of Honiton is surrounded by high, almost wall-like, hills and on top of one of them there is an unusual feature, a landmark that many fail to notice when speeding, only yards from it, to or from the direction of Axminster...

"On Honiton hill is an obelisk in the Italian style, eighty feet in height, erected by the late Bishop of Landaff [sic], *Dr Copplestone."* This was written in a late Victorian guide book to the Honiton district and here are just a few details about it.

In 1800 Edward Copleston, at the age of 24, became the Rector of Offwell, and was a man of modest means at that time. On 1 January 1800 his personal fortune amounted to £21 once all debts had been taken into consideration. Four years later he handed the living to his younger brother, John Gaius Copleston, whilst he took up the position of Provost and Dean of St Paul's. He next moved north to become Dean of Chester and later became the Bishop of Llandaff. Having accumulated a personal fortune he was able to indulge in building Offwell House (1828), the old Rectory (1845), the school and, in addition to much else, the impressive tower or folly (1843). Someone with more imagination than a knowledge of the local topography wrote a letter to the editor of the *Sunday Times* in March 1935 on the subject of follies stating that Bishop Copleston *" ... built the tower in order that he might be able to view his See* [diocese] *from afar!"* Although there is a terrific view from there, Llandaff, some 50 miles or more due north, is well out of sight. This amazing structure would have had to be of immense height to have peered over the shoulders of the Blackdowns and the Quantocks and gazed beyond the silvery-shining waters of the 'Severn Sea' (Bristol Channel) to the shores of South Wales. The Bishop, a confirmed bachelor, died in 1849, at the age of 73, and is buried in his cathedral 'across the water'. By stark contrast his brother John Gaius Copleston, Rector of Offwell until 1841, left his mark on the area with his twelve children!

During the Second World War the Home Guard availed themselves of the fine lookout facility that this landmark possesses. However some locals pondered the question of how wise it was to be stuck up the tower if there was a surprise enemy attack.

And so we have briefly looked at and wandered, almost at will, about this wonderful East Devon town so steeped in history and so packed and stacked with antiques. Unlike many small towns of a similar size its shopping centre thrives. Despite the frequent fires and the occasional setbacks, Honiton seems to go from strength to strength. Its name, because of its long association with lace, makes it famous the world over. Long may the town continue to prosper!